B293

5. White Sails on the Sea

M.A.W.

6. Fuzzy Wuzzy

M.A.W.

7. Polly, Pretty Polly

American Folk Song

M.A.W.

8. My Old Grey Mare

American Folk Song

M.A.W.

2. When I got there she got tired. *(3 times)*
   She laid down in an old court-yard.
3. Then they began to sing and pray *(3 times)*
   She jumped up and ran away.

Urbana June 1974

9. Cajun Folk Song

Louisianna Folk Song

M.A.W.

Urbana Oct. 1974

B293

10. Fiddle Dee Dee

English - American Folk Song

M.A.W.

Budapest May 1972

11. Deedle, Deedle Dumpling

English - American Folk Song

M.A.W.

Budapest May 1972

12. Sally Go Round the Sun

Children's Folk Song

M.A.W.

Urbana 1973

13. Madame, I Have Gold and Silver

American Folk Song

M.A.W.

Budapest 1972

14. What'll We Do with the Baby

Kentucky Folk Song

M.A.W.

Budapest 1972

B293

15. Going Down to Cairo

Ohio River Folk Song

M.A.W.

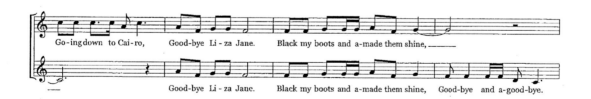

B293

For the University of Illinois Boys' Choir - Urbana June 1974

B293

16. Soldier, Soldier

North Carolina Folk Song

M.A.W.

B293

Budapest 1972

17. Go Tell Aunt Rhody

American Folk Song

M.A.W.

Budapest 1972

B293

18. Putman's Hill

Virginia Folk Song

M.A.W.

© Copyright Oxford University Press
Used by permission.

B293

Budapest 1972

19. Betty Ann

American Folk Song

M.A.W.

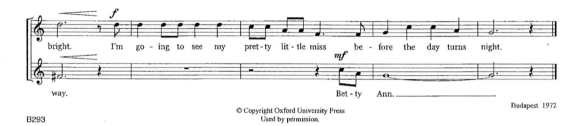

Budapest 1972

20. Buttermilk Hill

American Revolution Folk Song

M.A.W.

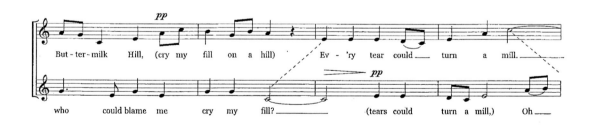

Székesfehérvar May 1972

21. Johnny Works with One Hammer

American Folk Song

M.A.W.

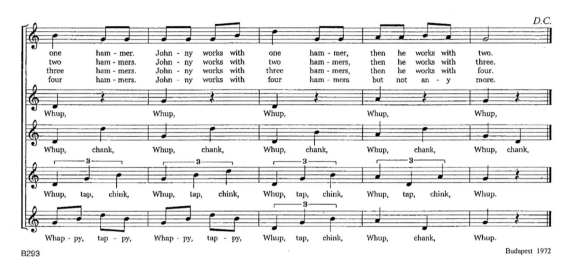

B293

Budapest 1972

22. Whistle, Daughter, Whistle

Appalachian Folk Song

M.A.W.

B293

San Antonio Oct. 1976

B293

23. One Morning in May

Virginia Folk Song

M.A.W.

San Antonio Oct. 1976

B293

24. Black Sheep

Southern U.S. Folk Song

M.A.W.

s,l, d r m s l

Urbana Feb. 1974

B293

where'd you leave your lamb?" "Way down ___ in the

where'd you leave your lamb?" ___ "Way down, down ___ in the

val - - ley." "Black sheep, Black sheep,

val - ley." My moth - er told me be - fore she went a - way, "Now

where's your lamb?" But I went out to play and the

take good care of the ba - by." And the

ba - by ran a - way ___ ran a - way. ___

ba - by ran a - way, and the poor lit - tle thing's cry - in' mom - my.

B293

25. A La Rueda de San Miguel

Mexican - American Folk Song

M.A.W.

s', *d r m s*

A la rue - da de San Mi-guel. A la rue - da de san Mi-guel

A la rue - da de San Mi - guel. To - des traen su ca - ja de miel.

A la rue - da de, a la rue - da de San Mi - guel, San Mi-guel.

A lo ma - du - ro, a lo ma - du - ro *(Ma - ri´- a) de bur - ro.

A lo ma - du - ro, A lo ma - du - ro. Que se vol - te´ a *(Ma - ri´- a) de bur - ro.

* substitute any name

Collected by Margaret Davis
Sung by Sr. Juanita, S H G Sept. 10, 1976

San Antonio Oct. 1976

B293